BusiWord

BusiWord

BUSINESS WORLD

BASEL OMAR ABU-ALI

authorHOUSE®

AuthorHouse™
1663 Liberty Drive
Bloomington, IN 47403
www.authorhouse.com
Phone: 1-800-839-8640

Published by AuthorHouse 11/10/2014

ISBN: 978-1-4969-4815-1 (sc)
ISBN: 978-1-4969-4814-4 (e)

Library of Congress Control Number: 2014918908

Contents

Part Four
Solutions

Dedication

This Book is dedicated to my amazing mother, soul of my father, wonderful brother, great sisters, and of course my lovely wife.

Preface

BusiWord is also dedicated to all seasoned business professionals and those who are taking their first steps exploring a business field and interested in learning more about it.

BusiWord is for:

- Accountants
- Advisors
- Analysts
- Controllers
- Consultants
- CxOs
- Directors
- Entrepreneurs
- Executives
- Government sector
- Investment bankers
- Investors
- MBA students
- Managers
- Owners
- Private sector
- Professionals
- Professional certificate students
- Professors
- Staff
- University students
- VPs
- People at all levels, anywhere, including *you!*

BusiWord includes 350 common business terms, concepts, models, and formulas from the accounting, finance, investment, management, economics, and marketing fields.

BusiWord provides an entertaining way for people in the business world to learn new terms and concepts or test their knowledge while enjoying solving crossword puzzles. It could also serve as a fun tool for executives looking for staff team-building activities. It's a fruitful use of time!

BusiWord can be solved in private, with a colleague, or within a group.

Introduction

This book consists of four parts:

Part One: Blank Crosswords

This section contains twenty-two crossword puzzles, beginning with crosswords that contain business terms, concepts, models, or formulas of three letters only. These words are mainly recognizable abbreviations, such as *IRR* (Internal rate of return).

The puzzles gradually progress from three-letter words to words of twenty-one or more letters.

The aim is to test your understanding of the correct term, concept, model, or formula suggested by the clues alongside the blank crossword. Fill in the words in the related blank squares until you complete the whole puzzle.

Part Two: Find the Word

This part contains ten completed crossword puzzles. The aim is to figure out which word belongs to each clue and scratch it out with your pen or pencil on the crossword. After finding all the words, you will end up with a few unused letters. Your next step is to figure out the missing word from these letters with the help of the clue given at the end of the puzzle. That clue—an international business school or university—is the same for each puzzle in this section. For example, the unused letters you end up with are T, U, H, and L. The solution is HULT.

Part Three: Shortcuts

This part contains selected shortcuts and summaries for major accounting, financial, and investment ratios ad concepts. This is a good quick reference and may help you in solving the puzzles.

Part Four: Puzzle Solutions

Each crossword, either blank or filled, contains different difficulty levels. If any of the words are new to you, then you have learned something new. If you already know the word(s), you have assessed your level of knowledge. In both cases, this can be used as a quick reference in the future.

All terms, concepts, models, and formulas were carefully reviewed and retrieved from major trusted professional business resources, references, and materials.

Hints:

- There is no space between words. Example: "BalanceSheet" instead of "Balance Sheet."
- The term can be spelled out or abbreviated. Example: "RiskFreeRate" or "RFR."
- The term can be one or two words. Example: "TurnoverRatio" or "Turnover."
- For each puzzle, you know the number of letters: three, seven, twelve, etc.
- On the blank crosswords, follow the reference number for each clue, either across or down.
- A clue can be specific or general. Example: "Stakeholders" is the clue, and the answer can be government or management or any other kind of stakeholders.

Good luck and have fun!

Part One

BLANK CROSSWORDS

Threes

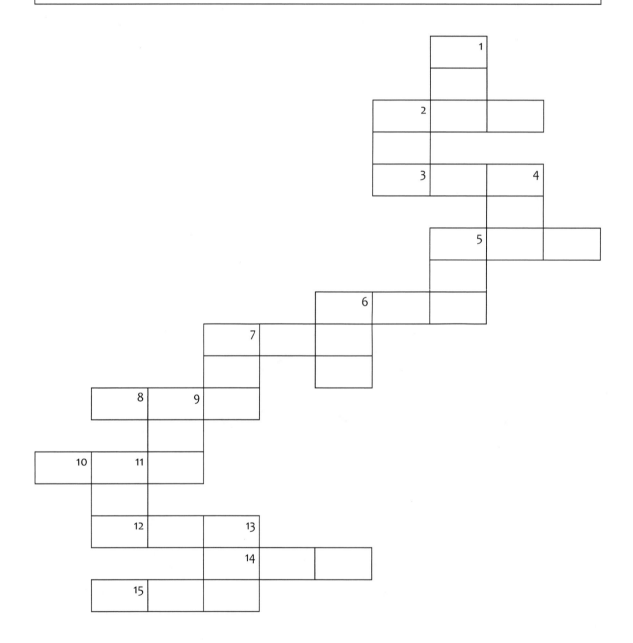

Across

2. Firm to go public

3. Rate of zero risk

5. By and to the government

6. Identify, decide, plan, and control firm's risks

7. Sum of discounted project's expected cash flows

8. Changes to equity from resources other than net profit

10. Valuation method

12. ROA × Financial Leverage

14. Options; the right to sell

15. Hardware, software, data, procedures, and people

Down

1. Total value of goods and services within the country's borders

2. NPV = 0

4. Assets Turnover × Net Profit Margin

5. Continuous improvements to deliver high-quality service

6. Invested Capital × Return Spread

7. Interest of subsidiary not owned by the parent company

9. Factors on which the strategy is dependent for its success

11. Firm's obligations to and for the community

13. Income over common stocks

Fours

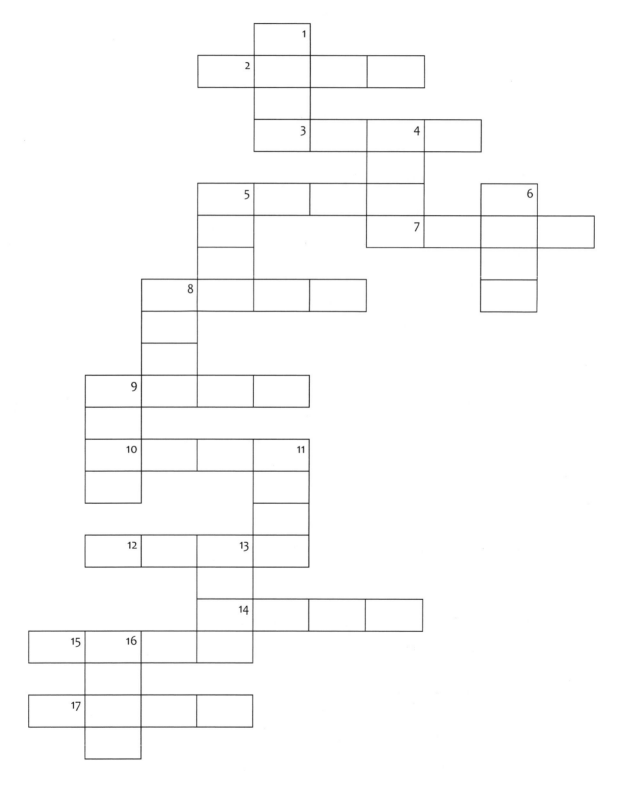

Across

2. US accounting reporting

3. In hand and at banks

5. Debt

7. Measures and metrics

8. Fixed income

9. Cost of equity

10. Asset that is not depreciated

12. Operating profit

14. Prepaid

15. Boston Consulting Group (BCG) Matrix

17. Business cycle stage

Down

1. Weighted cost of debt and equity

4. Unavoidable cost

5. Inventory accounting

6. Inventory accounting

8. Systematic risk

9. Options; the right to buy

11. Liability

13. International accounting reporting

16. Selling, general, and administrative expenses

Fives

Across

4. Objectives are

6. Determined by supply and demand

7. Alternative investments

9. Relationship between two or more variables

11. 7S framework

12. Market mix

13. Reward to employees

14. SMART

15. Formal review of firm's financial records

Down

1. Capital or operating

2. Derivatives

3. 7S framework

5. London banks' internal borrowing

8. Porter generic strategy

10. History analysis

11. Boston Consulting Group (BCG) Matrix

13. Name, term, design, sign, or symbol

Sixes

Across

2. Government policy in the market

6. Belbin team role

7. Integrity and moral

8. Elasticity of

11. Marco environmental factors

15. Industry life-cycle stage

16. Liabilities + Equity

Down

1. Product life-cycle stage

3. Assets – Liabilities

4. Continuous improvement

5. Before interest, taxes, depreciation, and amortization

9. Firm A + Firm B = Firm A or Firm B

10. General statement and guideline

12. Business cycle stage

13. Plan expressed in monetary term

14. Trade restriction

Sevens

Across

2. Bond; coupon rate > market rate

4. Statutory

6. Derivatives

10. Auditor opinion; statements are not presented fairly

12. 7S framework

14. Share price over EPS

16. Derivatives

17. Assets transferred to secure debt

Down

1. de Bono

2. Market mix

3. Limit the risk by purchasing opposite positions

5. Deferred

7. SWOT analysis

8. Trade restrictions

9. Retirement

11. Rent

13. Shareholders' contribution

15. Product life-cycle stage

Eights

Across

1. Accrual

3. Financing cost

5. Is the king

10. Boston Consulting Group (BCG) Matrix

11. Stated legal amount

12. Ratios; firms' ability to meet long-term obligations

16. Intangibles; infinite life

19. Stars, cash cows, dogs, and ?

20. 7S framework

22. Bond; coupon rate < market rate

23. Ratios; efficiency in utilizing assets

24. Central bank policy in the market

Down

2. Derivatives

4. Actual vs. Budget results analysis

5. Maximum ability for a firm to produce

6. Stock repurchased by the company

7. Solvency

8. In the short run, if price < average variable cost

9. Single-firm market structure

13. Bonds can be

14. Indirect costs and expenses

15. Assets – Debt

17. 3.4 defective parts per million

18. Process of setting goals and how to achieve them

21. Leadership style

Nines (Puzzle 1)

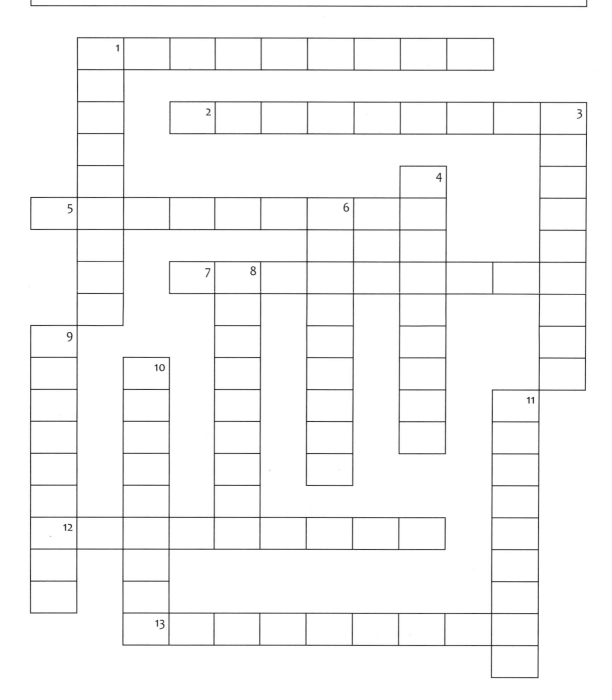

Across

1. Bond risk, related to government

2. Net Equity Value

5. Do not vary with output

7. Declared and distributed

12. Finished goods

13. Stakeholders

Down

1. Stakeholders

3. Business cycle stage

4. SWOT analysis

6. Few firms and high barriers to entry

8. Persistent increase in the price level over time

9. Market mix

10. The rumors and gossip network

11. Exclusive rights to sell a specified good or service

Nines (Puzzle 2)

Across

2. Investment; using equity method

7. Can be internally or externally, equity or debt

8. Liabilities over assets

10. Business cycle stage

13. Share Price × Number of Shares

14. Stakeholders

15. Auditor opinion; exceptions to accounting principles

Down

1. Valuation method

3. Days of (Inventory + Receivables – Payables)

4. Selling receivables to third party

5. Negative inflation rate

6. Ethics

9. Bank short-term facility

11. Stakeholders

12. Ratios; firm's ability to meet short-term obligations

Tens (Puzzle 1)

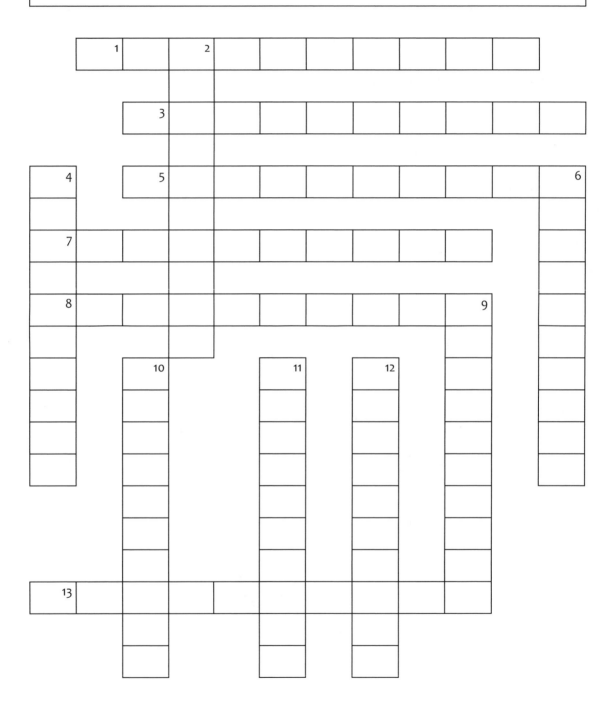

Across

1. Goodwill; drop in value

3. After-tax interest rate

5. Alternative investments

7. EV over EBITDA

8. Fraud triangle

13. Bond risk; changes in expected interest rates

Down

2. Written documents to support policies

4. Belbin team role

6. Doing the thing right

9. Investment; control with significant influence

10. Two or more shares for one

11. Relationship between a quantity demanded and price

12. Analysis, as a percentage of sales

Tens (Puzzle 2)

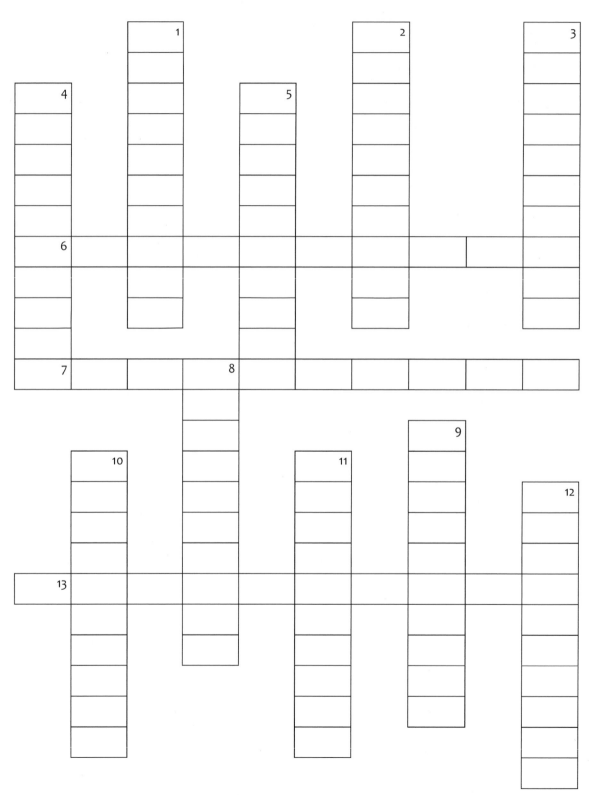

Across

6. Stakeholders

7. Rival

13. Leadership style

Down

1. Inability to pay debt

2. When auditors are unable to express an opinion

3. When a firm is unable to meet debt obligations

4. Market risk

5. Goodwill

8. Minimum price set by the government

9. Systematic risk

10. Production, sales, marketing, delivery, and service

11. Stakeholders

12. (Current Assets – Inventory) over Current Liabilities

Tens (Puzzle 3)

Across

6. Valuation method

8. Cost of specific basket of goods relative to base year

10. ROE × Retention Rate

11. To minimize inventory levels and cost

Down

1. The ability to influence others to attain goals

2. Share is; calculated price < market price

3. Preferred stocks can be

4. Null or alternative

5. SWOT analysis

7. Discount rate

9. Leadership style

Elevens

Across

1. Enterprise Value – Debt

6. Presents owner equity in the company

7. Time value of money

10. More responsibilities to front-line employees

11. Debit and credit

13. Firm A + Firm B = Firm A and Firm B

15. Share is; calculated price > market price

20. Inventory

21. Belbin team role

22. Fixed Cost over {unit (Selling Price – Variable Cost)}

23. Porter's five forces

Down

2. Assets – Equity

3. Preferred stocks can be

4. Alternative Investments

5. Contracting out business process by third party

8. Depreciation method

9. Belbin team role

12. Company's sales over total market or industry sales

14. Share Price × Number of Shares

16. Interest

17. Auditor; clean opinion

18. Sales – Cost of Goods Sold

19. Porter's five forces

Twelves (Puzzle 1)

Across

3. People not working or seeking jobs

8. Rate of zero risk

10. Decrease in the inflation rate over time

11. Firm-specific risk

12. Decision-making tool over three to five years

13. Two or more firms cooperate in one investment

14. CAPM

Down

1. Comparing firm's performance with the best in the market

2. Allocating fixed asset cost over its useful life

4. Depreciation of intangible assets

5. Assets – Liabilities

6. Maximum price set by the government

7. Depreciation method

9. Plan to generate profits includes merger, acquisition, and IPO

Twelves (Puzzle 2)

Across

6. Vary with output

9. Product life-cycle stage

13. Terminal value

14. Investigation process to evaluate a business

Down

1. Strengths, weaknesses, opportunities, and threats

2. The longest path through a network

3. Current assets over current liabilities

4. Assets = Liabilities + Equity

5. Marco environmental factors

7. Time value of money

8. Product-market strategy

10. Hurdle rate

11. Many firms and differentiated products

12. Operating Budget + Financial Budget

Thirteens

Across

2. SWOT analysis

6. Incentives, opportunities, and rationalizations

8. Value creation, profits, and logic behind

12. (1 – Dividend Payout ratio)

13. To produce ideas for a particular problem

14. Unusual and infrequent

18. Ratios; a firm's ability to generate income

19. Number of years required to cover project investment

20. Dividends per share over market price

21. Price of goods and services within the firm's units

22. Inventory

Down

1. Plan to obtain, expand, or replace physical facilities

3. Value after discounted period

4. Operations redesigning from scratch

5. Initial high price for product or service

7. Number of persons under one manager

9. Can be liquidated within one year or less

10. Direct investment

11. Certain layer of the market

15. Continuous budget

16. Firm A + Firm B = Firm C

17. Doing the right thing

Fourteens

Across

3. Bond pays no interest

4. Sensitivity analysis

5. Current Assets – Current Liabilities

8. Stock; with fixed par value and fixed dividend payout

12. Sales over assets

13. Groups meet to discuss quality problems and control

Down

1. Assets Turnover × Net Profit Margin

2. Porter generic strategy

6. Using generic methods to find solutions for a problem

7. New shares distribution

9. Dividends per share over EPS

10. Days of (Inventory + Receivables)

11. ROA × Financial Leverage

Fifteens

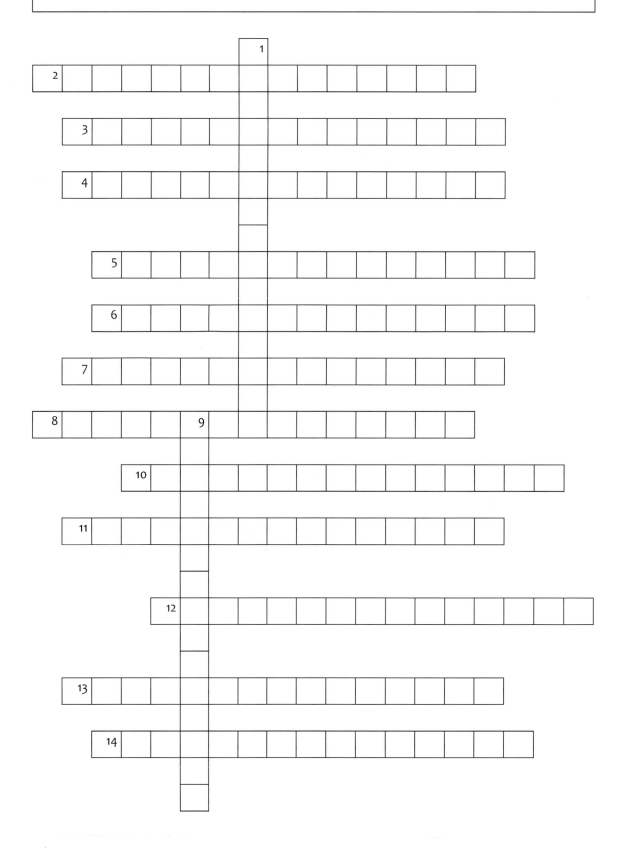

Across

2. Short-term (<270 days) money market security

3. Net profit over sales

4. Market Cap. + Market Value of Debt – Cash

5. EBIT

6. Budget prepared from scratch

7. Activity, liquidity, profitability, and solvency

8. Activities do not show on the balance sheet

10. Product-market strategy

11. Cost of the best alternative forgone

12. Sum of discounted project's expected cash flows

13. Purchase on credit

14. Sales – Cost – Expenses

Down

1. Porter generic strategy

9. Purchase of company by investor using debt

Sixteens

Across

2. Explains purpose, why company exists

3. The good, the bad, and the ugly

9. EBIT over interest

13. Private equity

14. Purchases over payables

15. Market study, technical study, and financial study

Down

1. Initiating a business, looking for new opportunities

4. Process of evaluating long-term capital projects

5. Cost advantage per additional unit of output

6. Mix of equity and debt financing for operations

7. Cumulative profits since inception

8. Fraud triangle

10. Income over common stocks

11. Leveraged buyout by management members

12. Elected by shareholders

Seventeens

38

Across

9. Quality, budget, and time

10. Selling; general and administrative expenses

Down

1. Financial, customer, process, learning, and innovation

2. COGS over inventory

3. Product-market strategy

4. Other comprehensive income

5. Product-market strategy

6. Assets over equity

7. Direct or indirect methods

8. Leverage; increases with fixed operating cost

Eighteens

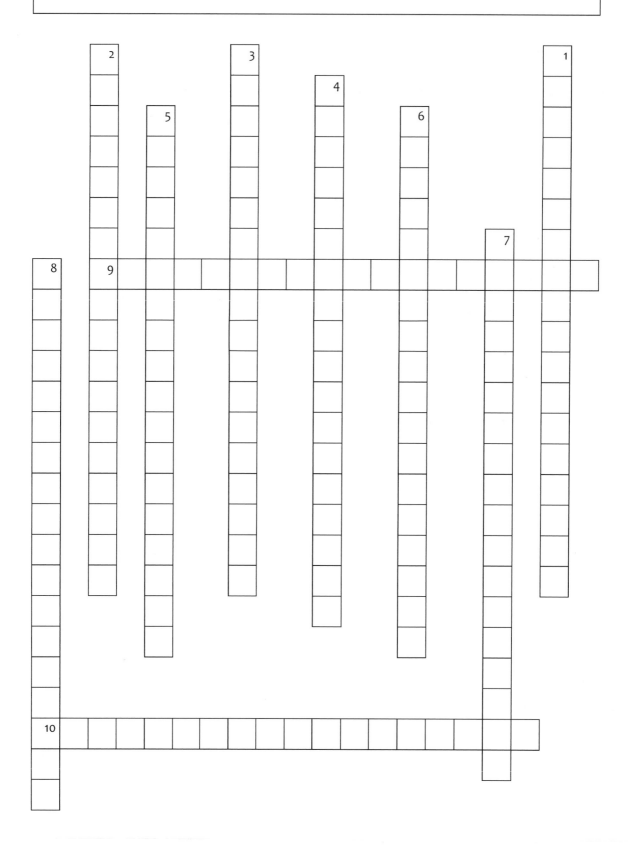

Across

9. Selling Price – Variable Cost

10. Invested Capital × Return Spread

Down

1. Other comprehensive income

2. Market structure

3. Analysis to estimate relationship between variables

4. Selling on credit

5. Due within one year or less

6. Consolidation

7. Present value of future cash flows over initial investment

8. Product-market strategy

Nineteens and Twenties

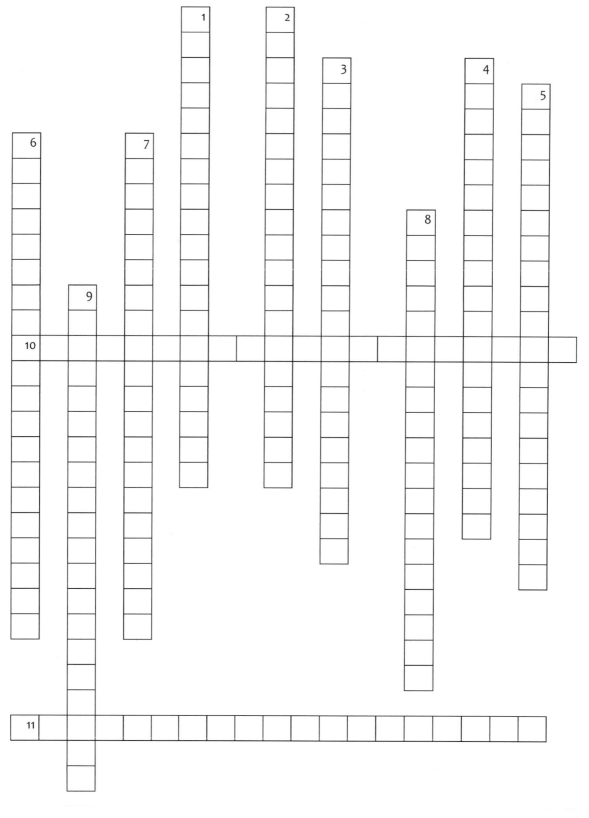

Across

10. Short-term instruments

11. Valuation method

Down

1. "What if" analysis

2. Balance sheet, income statement, and cash flow statement

3. NPV = 0

4. Net sales over receivables

5. An advantage an organization has over its rivals

6. Marketable securities

7. Total value of goods and services within the country's borders

8. Processes by which firms are controlled and directed

9. Staff evaluation

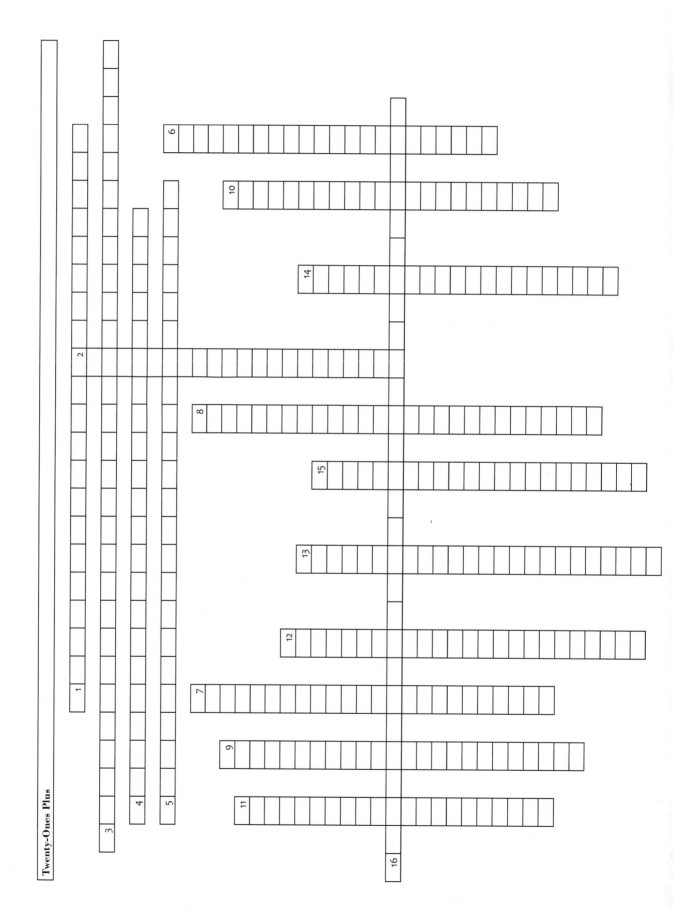

Twenty-Ones Plus

44

Across

1. ROE × Retention Rate

3. Firm's obligations to and for the community

4. Factors on which the strategy is dependent for its success

5. Depreciation allowance over years

16. Weighted cost of debt and equity

Down

2. Expenses to find and create new service or product

6. Continuous improvements to deliver high-quality service

7. Measures and metrics

8. Hardware, software, data, procedures, and people

9. Changes to equity from resources other than net profit

10. Interest of subsidiary not owned by the parent company

11. Keisen

12. Cost of equity

13. Identify, decide, plan, and control firm's risks

14. Stars, cash cows, dogs, and ?

15. Fixed Cost over {unit (Selling Price − Variable Cost)}

Part Two

FIND THE WORD

Threes and Fours

Solution clue: International business school or university

Across

- Option; the right to buy
- Total value of goods and services within the country's borders
- Fixed income
- Operating profit
- Firm's obligations to and for the community
- International accounting reporting
- Systematic risk
- Inventory accounting
- In hand and at banks
- Assets Turnover × Net Profit Margin
- Cost of equity
- Interest of subsidiary not owned by the parent company
- Prepaid
- By and to the government
- Invested Capital × Return Spread
- NPV = 0
- Unavoidable cost
- Asset that is not depreciated
- Inventory accounting
- Selling, general, and administrative expenses

Down

- US accounting reporting
- Liability
- Purchase of company by investor using debt
- Valuation method
- Factors on which the strategy is dependent for its success
- Weighted cost of debt and equity
- Hardware, software, data, procedures, and people
- Firm to go public
- Identify, decide, plan, and control firm's risks
- Changes to equity from resources other than net profit
- ROA × Financial Leverage
- Options; the right to sell
- Sum of discounted project's expected cash flows
- Rate of zero risk
- Continuous improvements to deliver high-quality service
- Income over common stocks
- Measures and metrics
- Debt
- Boston Consulting Group (BCG) Matrix
- Business cycle stage

Fives and Sixes

Solution clue: International business school or university

Across

- Government policy in the market
- Assets – Liabilities
- Firm A + Firm B = Firm A or Firm B
- Formal review of firm's financial records
- Porter generic strategy
- Alternative investments
- Capital or operating
- Name, term, design, sign, or symbol
- Integrity and morality
- Belbin team role
- Relationship between two or more variables
- Boston Consulting Group (BCG) Matrix
- Marco environmental factors
- SMART
- 7S framework
- History analysis

Down

- London banks internal borrowing
- Liabilities + Equity
- Trade restriction
- Continuous improvement
- Before interest, taxes, depreciation, and amortization
- Industry life-cycle stage
- Reward to employees
- Elasticity of
- Derivatives
- Plan expressed in monetary term
- Business cycle stage
- Determined by supply and demand
- Objectives are
- General statement and guideline
- Product life-cycle stage
- 7S framework
- Market mix

Sevens and Eights

Solution clue: International business school or university

Across

- Maximum ability for a firm to produce
- Deferred
- SWOT analysis
- Stated legal amount
- Shareholders' contribution
- Single-firm market structure
- Assets transferred to secure debt
- Accrual
- 1de Bono
- Solvency
- Process of setting goals and how to achieve them
- Derivatives
- 3.4 defective parts per million
- Bond; coupon rate < market rate
- Belbin team role
- Derivatives
- Days of (Inventory + Receivables – Payables)
- Is the king
- Rent
- Stock repurchased by the company
- Boston Consulting Group (BCG) Matrix
- Assets – Debt
- Financing cost

Down

- 7S framework
- Bonds can be
- Share price over EPS
- Stars, cash cows, dogs, and ?
- Central bank policy in the market
- Retirement
- Limit the risk by purchasing opposite positions
- In the short run; if price < average variable cost
- Actual vs. budget results analysis
- Derivatives
- Intangibles; infinite life
- Product life-cycle stage
- 7S framework
- Statutory
- Ratios; firms' ability to meet long-term obligations
- Ratios; efficiency in utilizing assets
- Trade restrictions
- Auditor opinion; statements are not presented fairly
- Indirect costs and expenses
- Leadership style
- Bond; coupon rate > market rate

Nines

Solution clue: International business school or university

Across

- Ethics
- Business cycle stage
- Auditor opinion; exceptions to accounting principles
- Few firms and high barriers to entry
- Valuation method
- Persistent increase in the price level over time
- Bank short-term facility
- Liabilities over assets
- Days of (Inventory + Receivables – Payables)
- Stakeholders
- Stakeholders
- Finished goods
- Declared and distributed
- Investment; using equity method
- Stakeholders
- Business cycle stage
- Bond risk; related to government

Down

- Do not vary with output
- Exclusive rights to sell a specified good or service
- Market mix
- Ratios; firm's ability to meet short-term obligations
- Negative inflation rate
- Can be internally or externally, equity or debt
- The rumors and gossip network
- Share Price × Number of Shares
- Net Equity Value
- Stakeholders
- SWOT analysis
- Selling receivables to third party

Tens

Solution clue: International business school or university

Across

- Leadership style

- (Current Assets – Inventory) over Current Liabilities

- When firm is unable to meet debt obligations

- Stakeholders

- ROE × Retention Rate

- Goodwill; drop in value

- Alternative investments

- Valuation method

- Belbin team role

- Bond risk; changes in expected interest rates

- Minimum price set by the government

- Fraud triangle

- Two or more shares for one

- Written documents to support policies

- nability to pay debt

- Null or alternative

- Cost of specific basket of goods relative to base year

- SWOT analysis

- Doing the thing right

- After tax interest rate

Down

- When auditors are unable to express an opinion

- Rival

- Discount rate

- Leadership style

- Share is; calculated price < market price

- Goodwill

- Preferred stocks can be

- The ability to influence others to attain goals

- Market risk

- EV over EBITDA

- Systematic risk

- Analysis; as a percentage of sales

- Production, sales, marketing, delivery, and service

- Investment; control with significant influence

- Relationship between a quantity demanded and price

- To minimize inventory levels and cost

- Stakeholders

Elevens

Solution clue: International business school or university

Across

- Sales – Cost of Goods Sold

- Assets – Equity

- Porter's five forces

- Depreciation method

- Share is; calculated price > market price

- Belbin team role

- Preferred stocks can be

- Alternative Investments

- Company's sales over total market or industry sales

Down

- Auditor; clean opinion

- Time value of money

- Belbin team role

- Interest

- Share Price × Number of Shares

- Porter's five forces

- Enterprise Value – Debt

- More responsibilities to frontline employees

- Presents owner equity in the company

- Debit and credit

- Contracting out business process by third party

- Firm A + Firm B = Firm A and Firm B

- Inventory

- Fixed Cost over {unit (Selling Price – Variable Cost)}

Twelves

Solution clue: International business school or university

Across

- Two or more firms cooperate in one investment

- Rate of zero risk

- Comparing firm's performance with the best in the market

- Many firms and differentiated products

- Strengths, weaknesses, opportunities, and threats

- Maximum price set by the government

- Vary with output

- People not working or seeking jobs

- Hurdle rate

- Product life-cycle stage

- Depreciation method

- Terminal value

Down

- The investigation process to evaluate a business

- Current assets over current liabilities

- Assets = Liabilities + Equity

- Marco environmental factors

- Plan to generate profits includes merger, acquisition, and IPO

- Decision-making tool over three to five years

- Decrease in the inflation rate over time

- Assets – Liabilities

- Product-market strategy

- The longest path through a network

- Operating Budget + Financial Budget

- Allocating fixed asset cost over its useful life

- Firm-specific risk

- Time value of money

- CAPM

- Depreciation of intangible assets

Thirteens and Fourteens

MARKETSEGMENT

RETENTIONRATE

STOCKDIVIDENDS

ROLLINGBUDGET

PRIVATEEQUITY

COSTLEADERSHIP

PROFITABILITY

TRANSFERPRICE

CAPITALBUDGET

BRAINSTORMING

REENGINEERING

Down words include: SPANOFCONTROL, QUALITYCIRCLES, DIVIDENDYIELD, TERMINALVALUE, DIVIDENDPAYOUT, EFFECTIVENESS, BUSINESSMODE, EXTRAORDINARY, OPPORTUNITIES, FRAUDTRIANGLE, PAYBACKPERIOD, RETURNONEQUITY, WORKINGCAPITAL, PRICEASSETS, CURRENTASSETS, CONSOLIDATION, RETURNONASSETS, MEASURESMODE

Solution clue: International business school or university

Across

- Certain layer of the market
- (1 – Dividend Payout ratio)
- New shares distribution
- Continuous budget
- Direct investment
- Porter generic strategy
- Ratios; firm's ability to generate income
- Price of goods and services within the firm's units
- Plan to obtain, expand, or replace physical facilities
- To produce ideas for a particular problem
- Operations redesigning from scratch

Down

- Unusual and infrequent
- Incentives, opportunities, and rationalizations
- Number of persons under one manager
- Doing the right thing
- SWOT analysis
- Value after discounted period
- Groups meet to discuss quality problems and control
- Dividends per share over market price
- Dividends per share over EPS
- Value creation, profits, and logic behind
- Number of years required to cover project investment
- Assets Turnover × Net Profit Margin
- ROA × Financial Leverage
- Can be liquidated within one year or less
- Current Assets – Current Liabilities
- Firm A + Firm B = Firm C
- Initial high price for product or service

Fifteens and Sixteens

NET PROFIT MARGIN

RETAINED EARNINGS

RATIONALIZATIONS

FEASIBILITY STUDY

ECONOMIES OF SCALE

OFF BALANCE SHEET

MISSION STATEMENT

INTEREST COVERAGE

LEVERAGED BUYOUT

NET PRESENT VALUE

CAPITAL BUDGET

OPPORTUNITY COST

MANAGEMENT BUYOUT

INCOME STATEMENT

ENTERPRISE VALUE

Solution clue: International business school or university

Across

- Net profit over sales

- Cumulative profits since inception

- Fraud triangle

- Market study, technical study, and financial study

- Cost advantage per additional unit of output

- Activities do not show on the balance sheet

- Explains why company exists

- EBIT over interest

Down

- Sum of discounted project's expected cash flows

- Activity, liquidity, profitability, and solvency

- Purchase of company by investor using debt

- Market Cap. + Market Value of Debt – Cash

- Process of evaluating long-term capital projects

- EBIT

- Porter's generic strategy

- Short-term (<270 days) money market security

- Purchases over payables

- Initiating a business, looking for new opportunities

- The cost of the best alternative forgone

- Mix of equity and debt financing for operations

- Purchase on credit

- Sales – Cost – Expenses

- Leveraged buyout by the management members

BOSTONCONSULTINGGROUP

KEYPERFORMA

CONTINUOUSIMPROVEMENT

INTERNALRATEOFRETURN

CASHFLOWSTATEMENT

GROSSDOMESTICPRODUCT

TOTALQUALITYMANAGEMENT

MARKETPENETRATION

ACCUMULATEDDEPRECIATION

CORPORATEGOVERN

BREAKEVENPOINTANAL

ENTERPRISERISKMANAGEMENT

PROFITABILITYINDEX

OPERATINGLEVERAGE

CONTRIBUTIONMAR

CRITICALSUCCESSFACTORS

CURRENTLIABILI

RESEARCHANDDEVELOP

(Down words: CONSERVATIVE, PENSIONOBLIGATION, HEDGINGDERIVATIVE, FINANCIALSTATEMENTS, FINANCIALLEVERAGE, PERFORMANCE, APPRAISAL)

CAPITALASSETPRICINGMODEL
NCEINDICATORS
OPERATINGEXPENSES
REGRESSIONANALYSIS
PROJECTMANAGEMENT
OTHERCOMPREHENSIVEINCOME
ANCE
YSIS
MARKETABLESECURITIES
GIN
INVENTORYTURNOVER
TIES
MENT
DISCOUNTEDCASHFLOWS
PRODUCTDEVELOPMENT
SHORTTERMINSTRUMENTS
NONCONTROLLINGINTEREST
RECEIVABLESTURNOVER
SUSTAINABLEGROWTHRATE
ACCOUNTSRECEIVABLE
BALANCEDSCORECARD
MARKETDEVELOPMENT
COMPETITIVEADVANTAGE
PERFECTCOMPETITION
ELIMINATIONENTRIES
SENSITIVITYANALYSIS

Solution clue: International business school or university

Across

- Other comprehensive income

- Balance sheet, income statement, and cash flow statement

- Other comprehensive income

- Assets over equity

- Staff evaluation

- "What if" analysis

- An advantage an organization has over its rivals

- Market structure

- Valuation method

- Consolidation

- Interest of subsidiary not owned by the parent company

- ROE × Retention Rate

- Net sales over receivables

- Selling on credit

- Product-market strategy

- Financial, customer, process, learning, and innovation

- Marketable securities

- Product-market strategy

Down

- Keisen
- Factors on which the strategy is dependent for its success
- Stars, cash cows, dogs, and ?
- Identify, decide, plan, and control firm's risks
- Total value of goods and services within the country's borders
- NPV = 0
- Depreciation allowance over years
- Continues improvements to deliver high-quality service
- Product-market strategy
- Direct or indirect methods
- Expenses to find and create new service or product
- Present value of future cash flows over initial investment
- Fixed cost over {unit (Selling Price – Variable Cost)}
- Leverage; increases with fixed operating cost
- Selling Price – Variable Cost
- Processes by which firms are controlled and directed
- Due within one year or less
- Measures and metrics
- Short-term instruments
- Analysis to estimate relationship between variables
- Cost of equity
- Changes to equity from resources other than net profit
- Quality, budget, and time
- Selling; general and administrative expenses
- COGS over inventory

Part Three

SHORTCUTS

Accounting Balance

Assets	Liabilities	Equity

Assets		

	Assets	Liabilities	Equity
+	−	+	+
−	+	−	−

Liabilities		

	Liabilities	Equity
+	−	−
−	+	+

Equity		

	Equity
+	−
−	+

Accounting Equation

Assets	=	Liabilities	+	Equity
=		=		=
Current Assets		Current Liabilities		Capital
+		+		+
Fixed Assets		Long Term Debt		Reserves
+				+
Intangibles				Returned Earnings
				+
				Revenue
				−
				Expenses
				−
				Dividends

Business Model Aspects

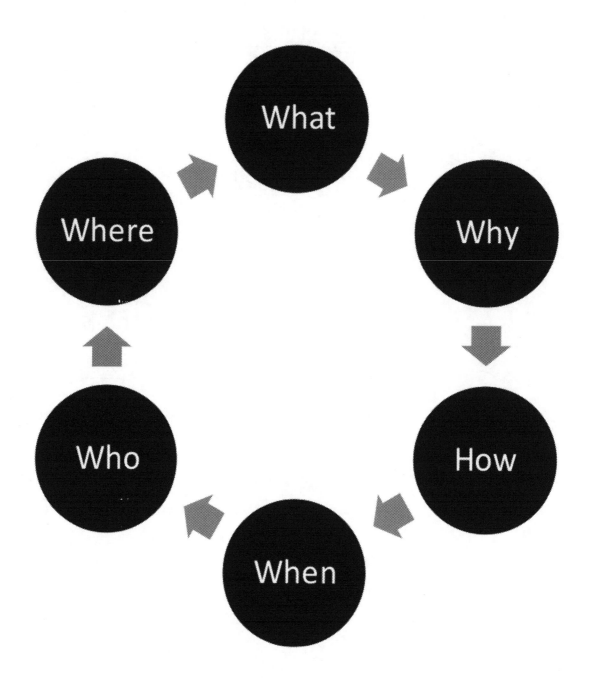

Capital Budgeting–Feasibility Study–Business Plan

Business Plan

=

Documentation

Feasibility Study   +

=

Capital Budgeting   +   Market Study

=   +

Financial Study   Technical Study

Cash Conversion Cycle

365

/

Receivables Turnover

Days of sales outstanding

+

Days of inventory in hand

=

Inventory Turnover

Operating Cycle

−

Payables Turnover

Days of payables

=

Cash Conversion Cycle

Earnings—Profit—Income

Sales
(COGS)
GP
(OPEX)
EBITDA
(DA)
EBIT
(I)
EBT
(T)
E

EBIT = **OP** = **OI**

E = **NP** = **NI**

/

#S
EPS

Free Cash Flow to Firm (FCFF) & Free Cash Flow to Equity (FCFE)

Net Profit	Net Profit
+	+
Noncash items (Depreciation)	Noncash items (Depreciation)
+	+
Interest (1–Tax)	
–	–
Changes in Working Capital	Changes in Working Capital
–	–
CAPEX	CAPEX
	+
	New (or repayment of) debt
+	+
TV	TV
=	=
FCFF	**FCFE**

Financial Analysis

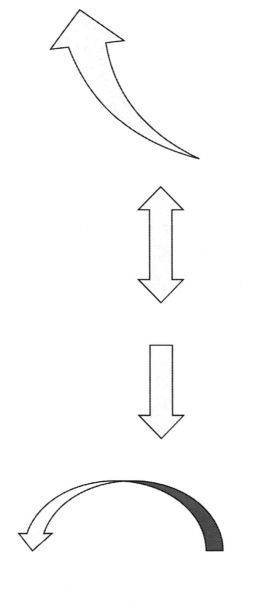

Common size (to sales)	Trend—History	Budget Variance	Forecast
Common size (to assets)	Last month/period	Benchmarking	DCF

Financial Ratios

(Cash + Marketable Securities)	Current Assets	(Current Assets – Inventory)	Total Assets	Total Liabilities	Cash Flow from Operations
Cash Ratio	(/) Liquidity Ratio (–) Working Capital	Quick Ratio		Debt Ratio	CFO / Assets
		Financial Leverage		Debt to Equity Ratio	CFO / Liabilities
					CFO / Interest

/

Total Assets
Current Liabilities
Equity
Interest

Net Profit | EBIT | Gross Profit | COGS | Purchases | Sales

Receivables Turnover

Inventory Turnover

Fixed Assets Turnover

Assets Turnover

Payables Turnover

Return on Assets

Return on Equity

Net Profit Margin

Gross Profit Margin | Operating Profit Margin

Interest Coverage Ratio

/

Receivables

Inventory

Fixed Assets

Total Assets

Payables

Equity

Sales

Interest

Goodwill

 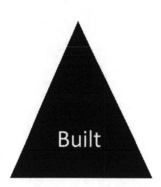 

Acquired

Built

Maintained

Investment Appraisal Indicators

	Payback Period (PBP)	Discounted PBP	Accounting Rate of Return (ARR)	Net Present Value (NPV)	Internal Rate of Return (IRR)	Profitability Index (PI)
Simple calculation	Y		Y			
Income approach			Y			
Cash flows approach	Y	Y		Y	Y	Y
Ignores cash flow after payback period	Y	Y				
Considers TVM		Y		Y	Y	Y
Discount rate		Y		Y	Y	Y
Terminal value	Y			Y	Y	Y
Results — # Years	Y	Y				
Results — Value				Y		
Results — %			Y		Y	
Results — >1<						Y

Key (Net Present Value or NPV) Value Drivers

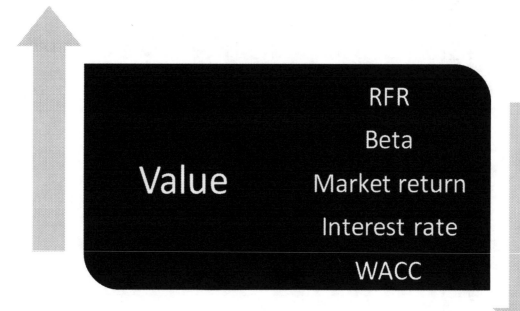

Mergers and Acquisitions

	Firm	Firm	Firm(s) Operating
Merger	A	+ B	= A or B
Acquisition	A	+ B	= A and B
Consolidation	A	+ B	= C
Joint Venture	A	+ B	= A and B and C

Multiples

Enterprise Value (EV)	Market Share Price	Dividends

/

Sales	EV to Sales	Price to Sales		
Book Value		Market to Book		
Earnings per Share (EPS)		Price to Earnings	Payout Ratio	
Market Share Price			Yield Ratio	
EBITDA	EV Multiple			

EV = Market Capitalization + Market Value of Debt – Cash

Market Cap. = Shares Outstanding × Market Share Price

EBITDA = Earnings before interest, taxes, depreciation, and amortization

Options

CALL	LONG	Owner	Buyer	Right to buy
	SHORT	Writer	Seller	Obligation to sell

PUT	LONG	Owner	Buyer	Right to sell
	SHORT	Writer	Seller	Obligation to buy

CALL	Market Price	>	Strike Price	In the money
	Market Price	=	Strike Price	At the money
	Market Price	<	Strike Price	Out of the money

PUT	Market Price	<	Strike Price	In the money
	Market Price	=	Strike Price	At the money
	Market Price	>	Strike Price	Out of the money

Option Value	=	Intrinsic Value (IV)	+	Time Value

=

CALL	Market Price – Strike Price
PUT	Strike Price – Market Price

=

Premium – IV

Price-Earnings Ratio (P/E Ratio)

$$\text{P/E} = \frac{\text{D/E}}{(K-G)} \qquad = \qquad P = \frac{D}{(K-G)} \qquad = \qquad K = \frac{D}{P} + G$$

$$E = EPS = \frac{\text{Net Income}}{\text{Common Shares}}$$

D:	Dividends
P:	Price
G:	Growth rate
K_e:	Cost of equity
K_d:	Cost of debt
W_e:	Weight of equity
W_d:	Weight of debt
RFR:	Risk-free rate
B:	Beta
MR:	Market return

$$G = (1 - \text{D/E}) \times \text{ROE}$$

$$\text{ROE} = \frac{\text{Assets}}{\text{Equity}} \times \frac{\text{Net Income}}{\text{Sales}} \times \frac{\text{Sales}}{\text{Assets}}$$

$$K = \text{Hurdle Rate} = \text{Discount Rate} = \text{WACC}$$

$$\text{WACC} = (K_e \times W_e) + (K_d \times W_d)$$

$$= \qquad\qquad = \qquad\qquad = \qquad\qquad =$$

$$\text{CAPM} \qquad \frac{\text{Equity}}{(\text{Equity} + \text{Debt})} \qquad \text{Interest} (1-\text{Tax}) \qquad \frac{\text{Debt}}{(\text{Equity} + \text{Debt})}$$

$$=$$

$$\text{RFR} + B (\text{MR} - \text{RFR})$$

S-Holders

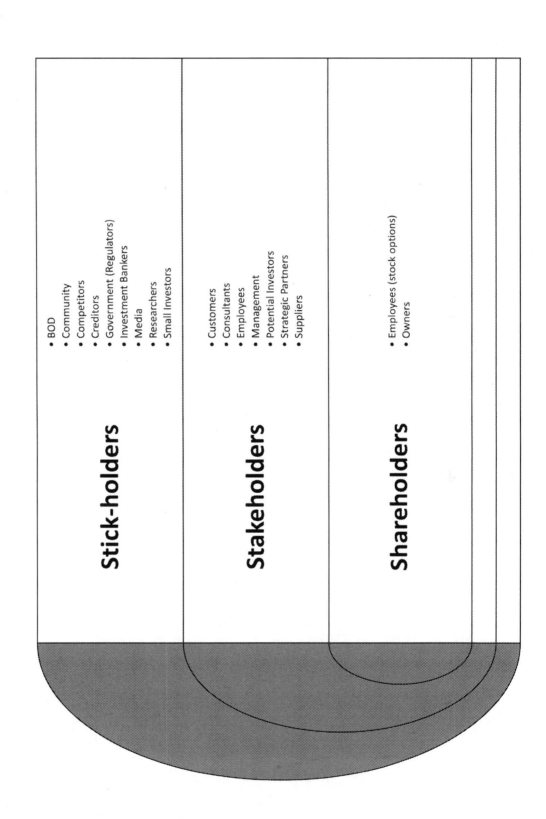

Stick-holders
- BOD
- Community
- Competitors
- Creditors
- Government (Regulators)
- Investment Bankers
- Media
- Researchers
- Small Investors

Stakeholders
- Customers
- Consultants
- Employees
- Management
- Potential Investors
- Strategic Partners
- Suppliers

Shareholders
- Employees (stock options)
- Owners

Part Four

SOLUTIONS

Threes

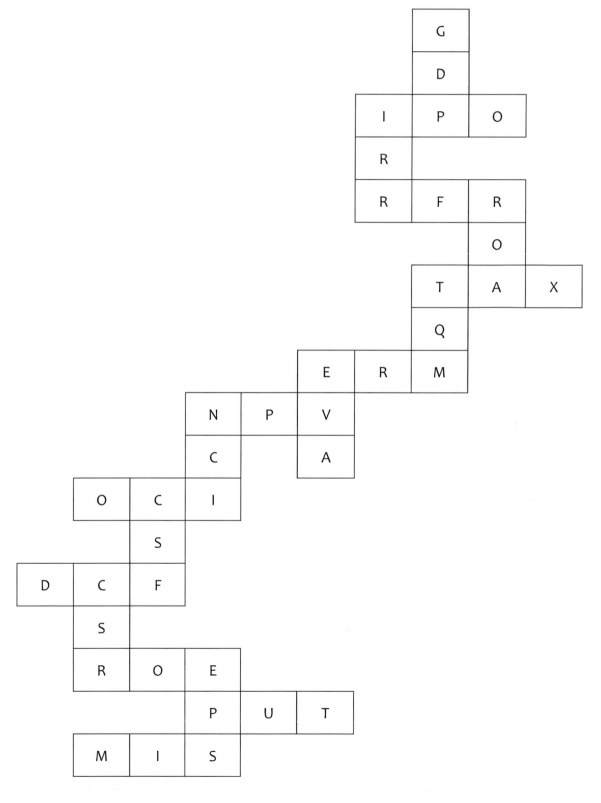

Fours

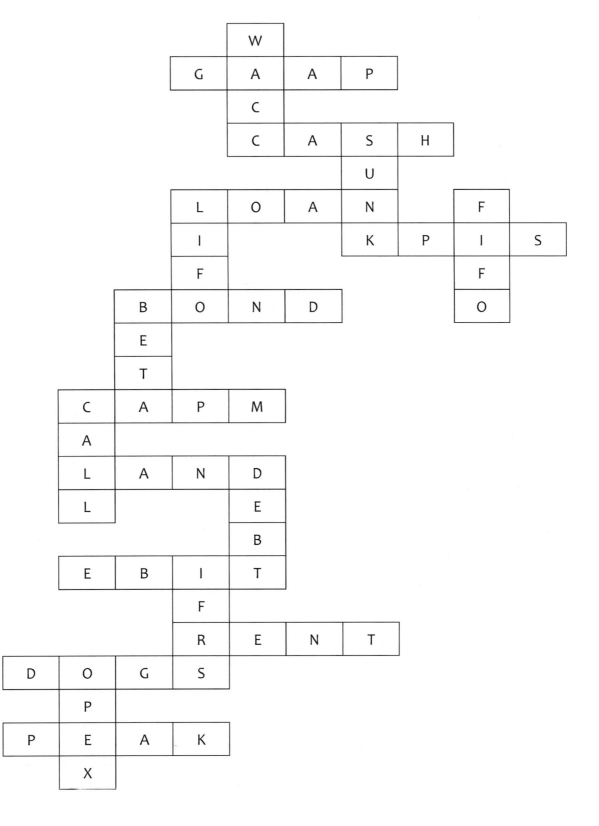

Fives

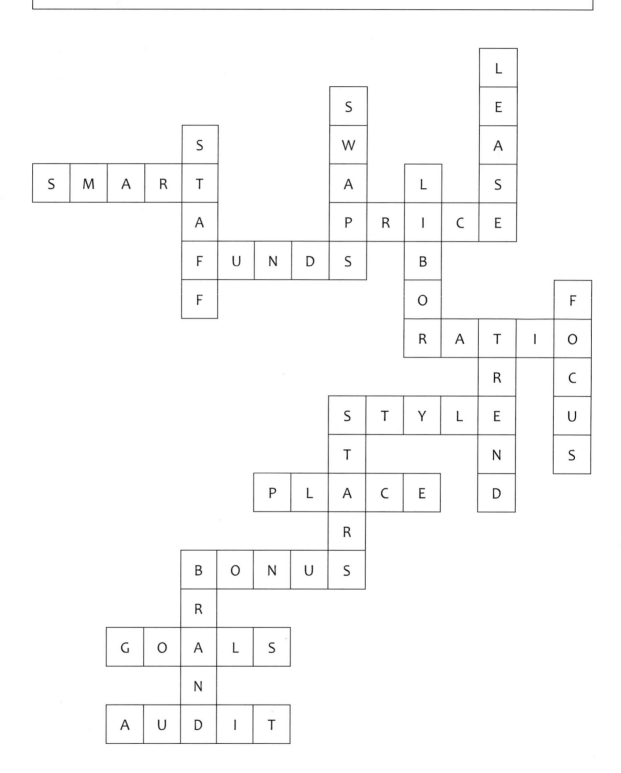

Sixes

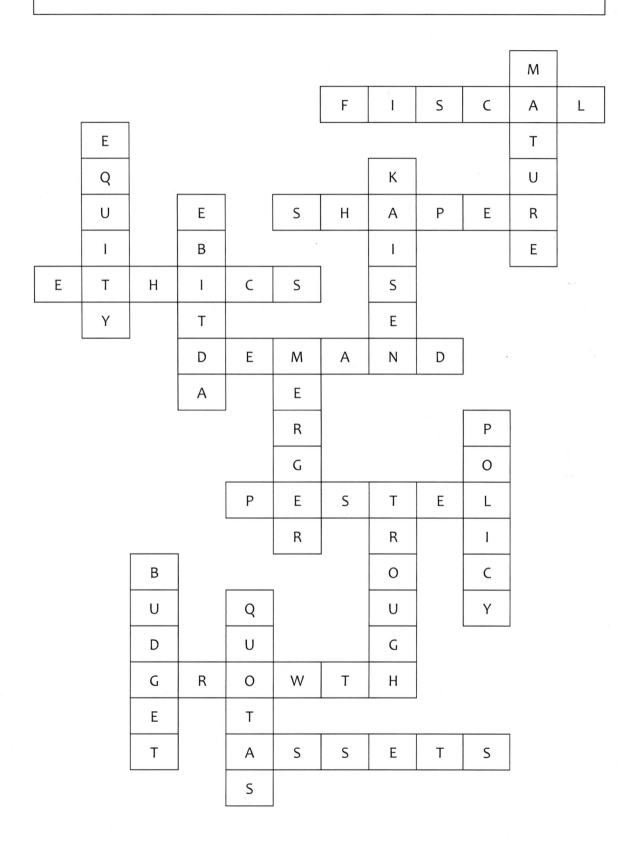

Sevens

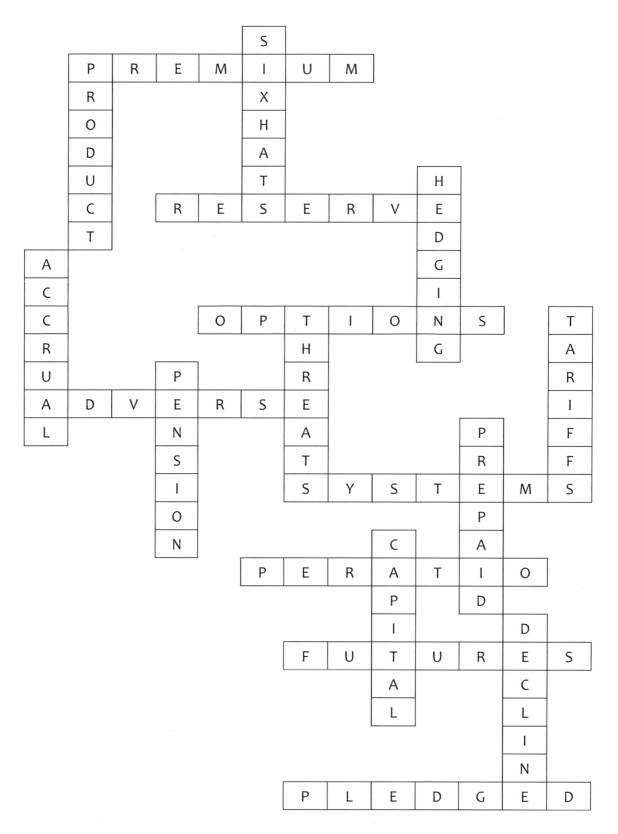

Eights

Nines (Puzzle 1)

	S	O	V	E	R	E	I	G	N	
S	U	P	P	L	I	E	R	S	
B	O	O	K	V	A	L	U	E
F	I	X	E	D	C	O	S	T
D	I	V	I	D	E	N	D	S
P	R	O	M	O	T	I	O	N
G	R	A	P	E	I	N	V	E	N	T	O	R	Y
E	M	P	L	O	Y	E	E	S
F	R	A	N	C	H	I	S	E

Nines (Puzzle 2)

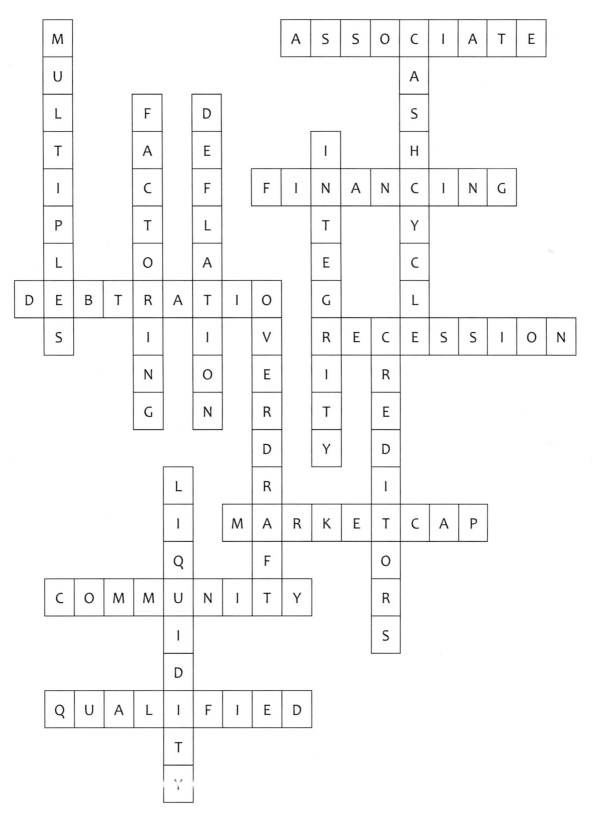

Tens (Puzzle 1)

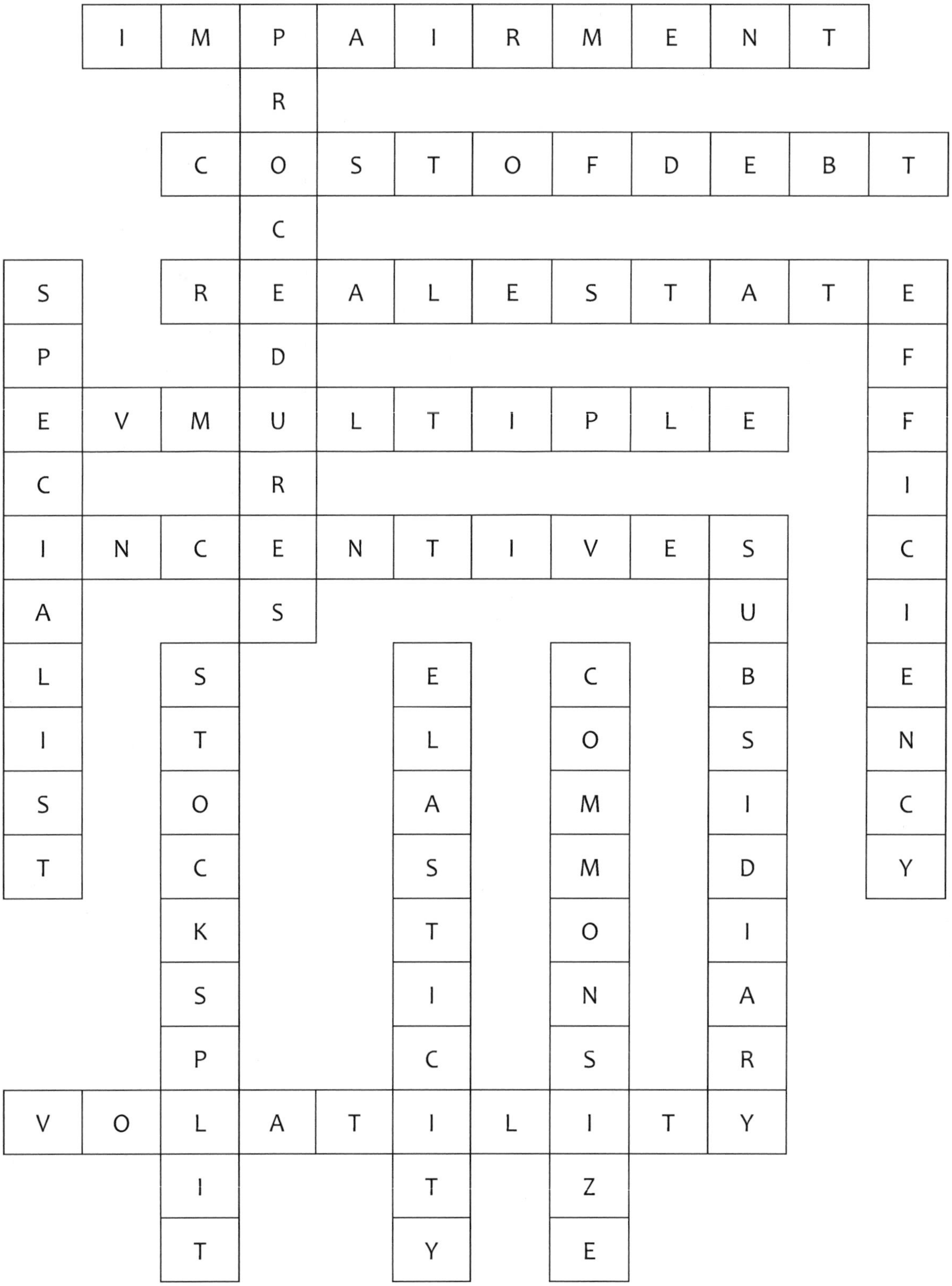
IMPAIRMENT
COSTOFDEBT
REALESTATE
EVMULTIPLE
INCENTIVES
VOLATILITY
PROCEDURES
SPECIALIST
EFFICIENCY
SUBSIDIARY
STOCKSPLIT
ELASTICITY
COMMONSIZE

Tens (Puzzle 2)

Tens (Puzzle 3)

OVERVALUED

LEADERSHIP

HYPOTHESIS

CUMULATIVE

WEAKNESSS

ASSET BASED

PRICE INDEX

HURDLE RATE

GROWTH RATE

AUTOCRATIC

JUST IN TIME

Elevens

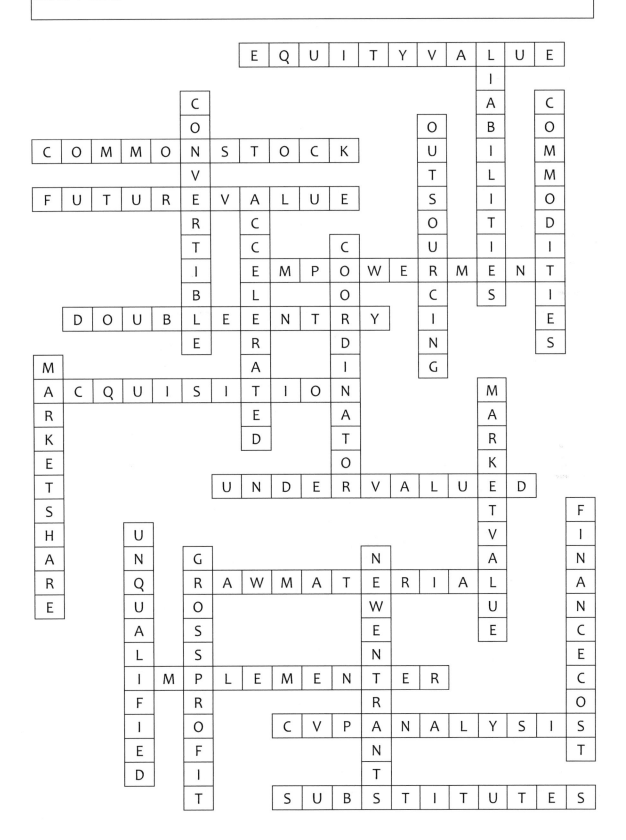

Twelves (Puzzle 1)

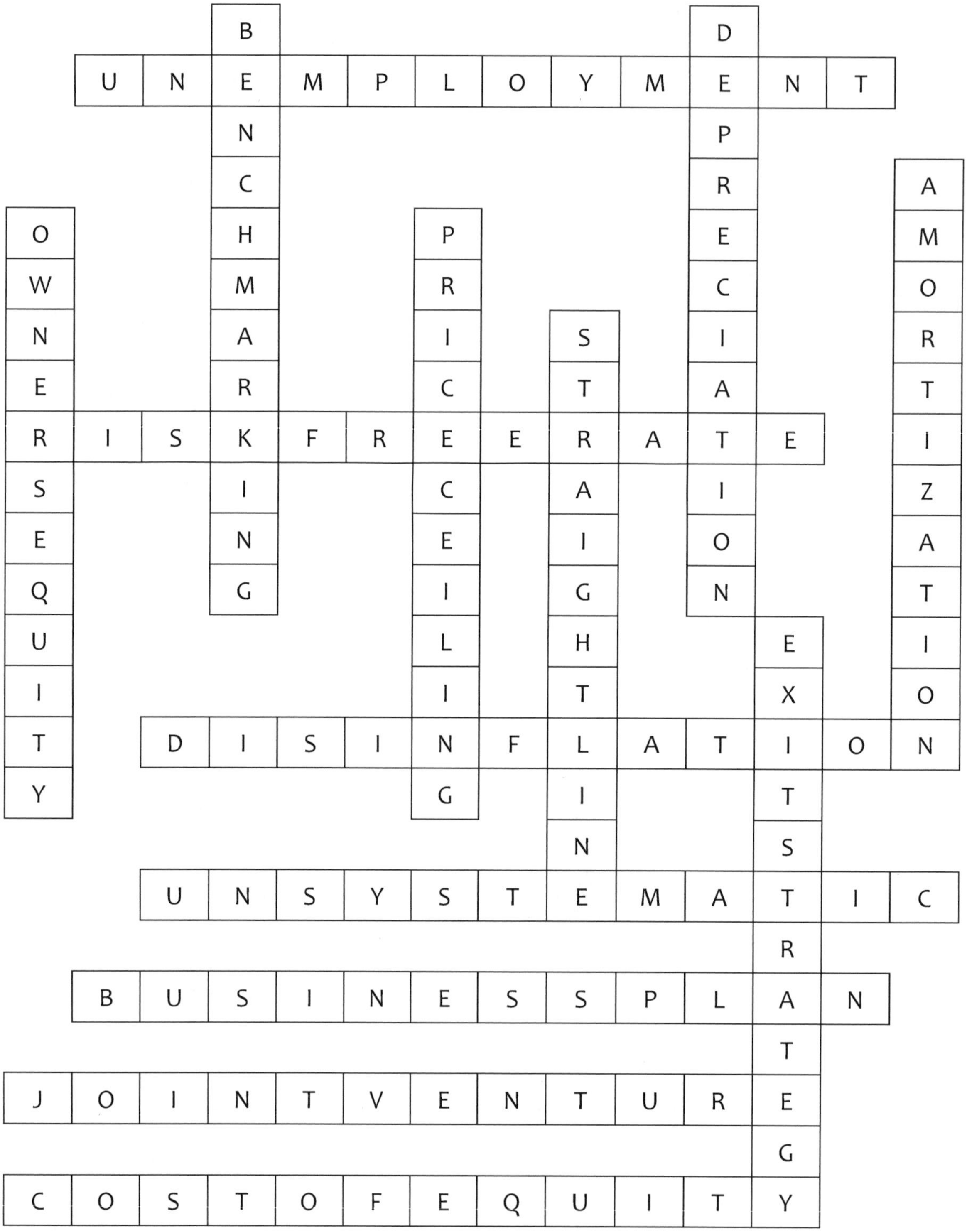
UNEMPLOYMENT
RISKFREERATE
DISINFLATION
UNSYSTEMATIC
BUSINESSPLAN
JOINTVENTURE
COSTOFEQUITY
BENCHMARKING
DEPRECIATION
AMORTIZATION
OWNERSEQUITY
PRICECEILING
STRAIGHTLINE
EXITSTRATEGY

Twelves (Puzzle 2)

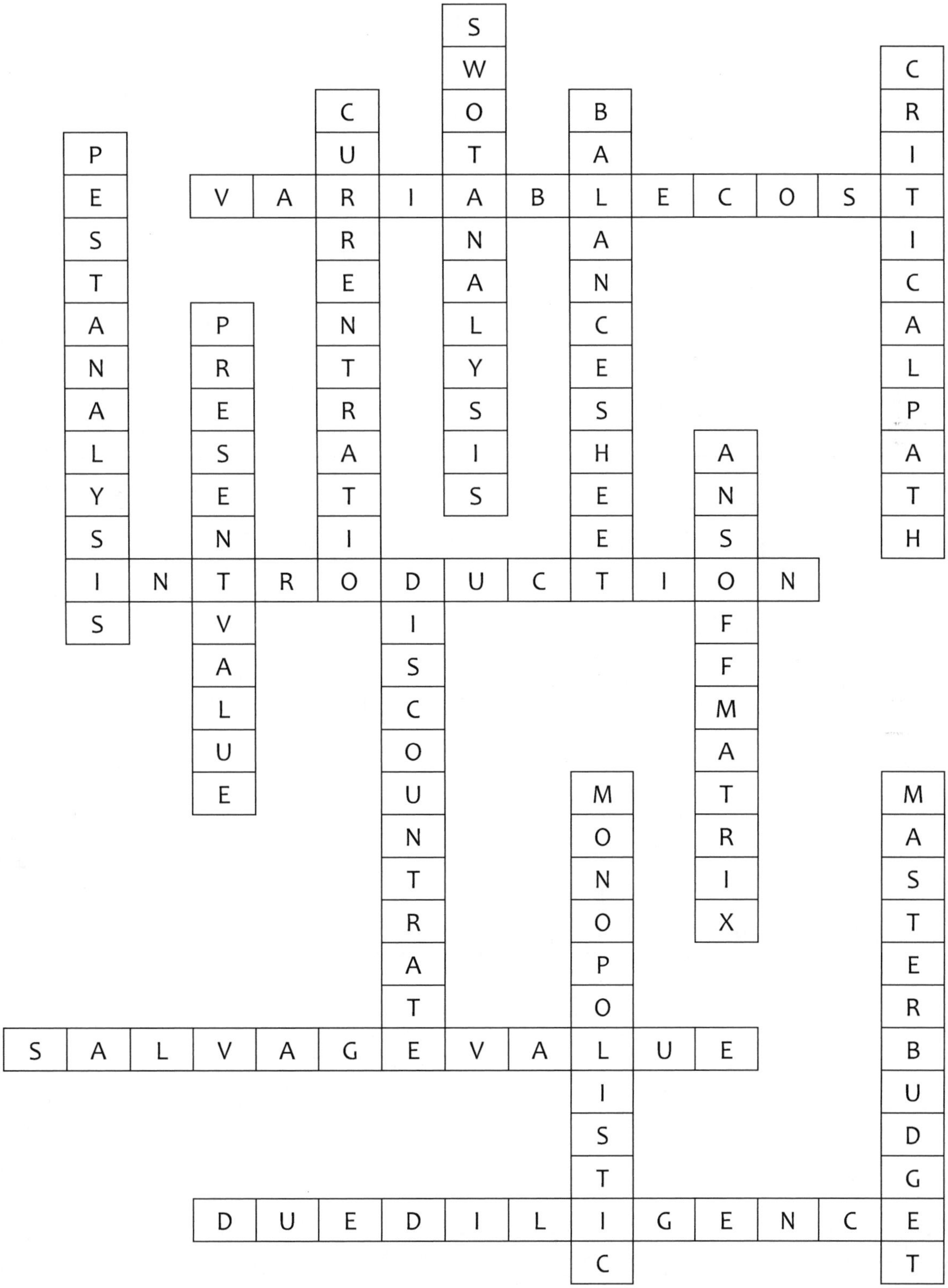
SWOTANALYSIS
CURRENTRATIO
BALANCESHEET
CRITICALPATH
PESTANALYSIS
VARIABLECOST
PRESENTVALUE
INTRODUCTION
DISCOUNTRATE
ANSOFFMATRIX
MONOPOLISTIC
MASTERBUDGET
SALVAGEVALUE
DUEDILIGENCE

Thirteens

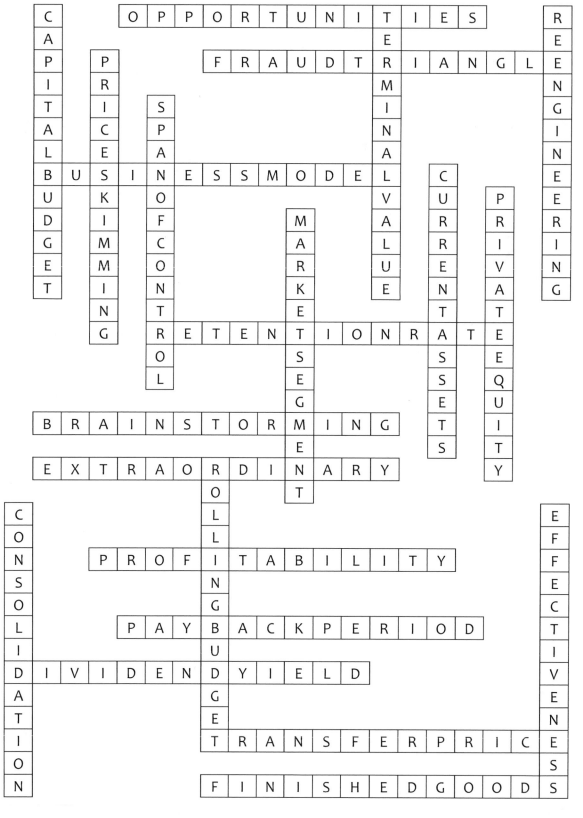

Fourteens

ZEROCOUPONBOND

WHATIFANALYSIS

WORKINGCAPITAL

PREFERREDSTOCK

ASSETSTURNOVER

QUALITYCIRCLES

Down words:
RETURNONASSETS
COSTLEADERSHIP
PROBLEMSOLVING
RETURNONEQUITY
DIVIDENDPAYOUT
STOCKDIVIDENDS
OPERATINGCYCLE

Fifteens

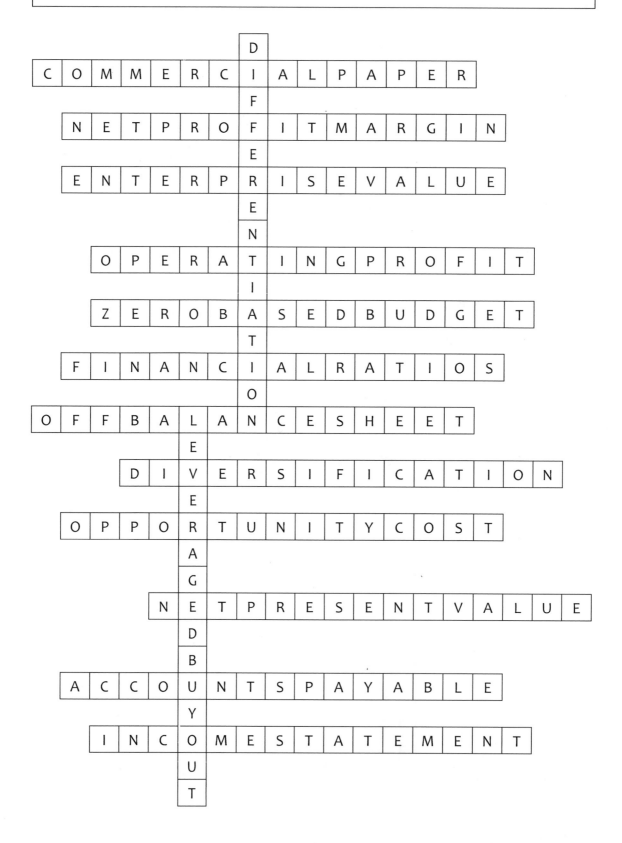

COMMERCIAL PAPER

NET PROFIT MARGIN

ENTERPRISE VALUE

OPERATING PROFIT

ZERO BASED BUDGET

FINANCIAL RATIOS

OFF BALANCE SHEET

DIVERSIFICATION

OPPORTUNITY COST

NET PRESENT VALUE

ACCOUNTS PAYABLE

INCOME STATEMENT

DIFFERENTIATION

LEVERAGED BUYOUT

Sixteens

MISSION STATEMENT

SCENARIO ANALYSIS

ENTREPRENEURSHIP

CAPITAL STRUCTURE

CAPITAL BUDGETING

INTEREST COVERAGE

RATIONALIZATIONS

ECONOMIES OF SCALE

RETAINED EARNINGS

EARNINGS PER SHARE

MANAGEMENT BUYOUT

BOARD OF DIRECTOR

DIRECT INVESTMENT

PAYABLES TURNOVER

FEASIBILITY STUDY

Seventeens

BALANCEDSCORECARD

INVENTORYTURNOVER

PENTIONOBLIGATION

MARKETPENETRATION

MARKETDEVELOPMENT

FINANCIALLEVERAGE

CASHFLOWSTATEMENT

OPERATINGLEVERAGE

PROJECTMANAGEMENT

OPERATINGEXPENSES

Eighteens

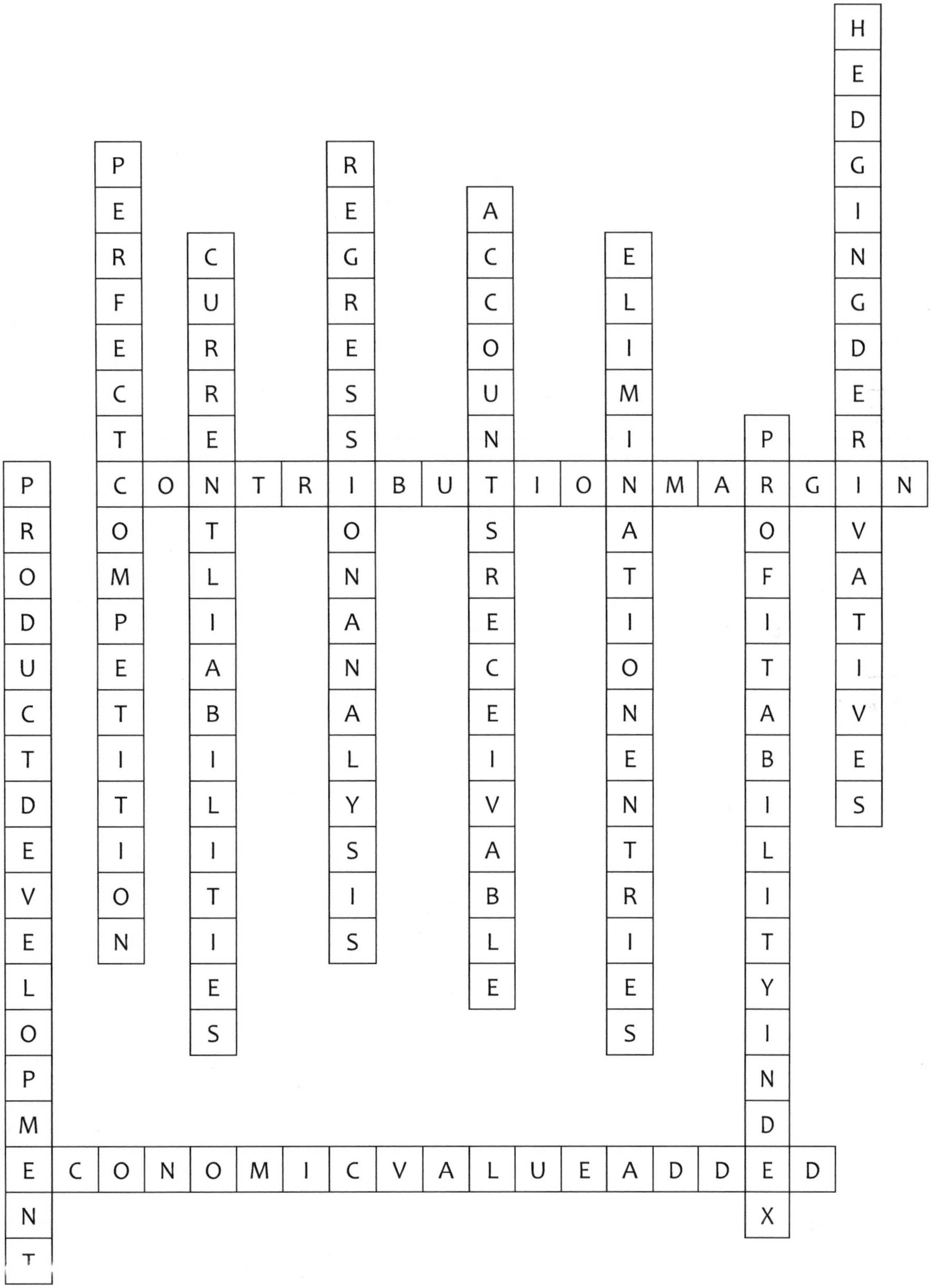
PERFECTCOMPETITION
CURRENTLIABILITIES
REGRESSIONANALYSIS
ACCOUNTSRECEIVABLE
ELIMINATIONENTRIES
HEDGINGDERIVATIVES
PRODUCTDEVELOPMENT
PROFITABILITYINDEX
CONTRIBUTIONMARGIN
ECONOMICVALUEADDED

Nineteens and Twenties

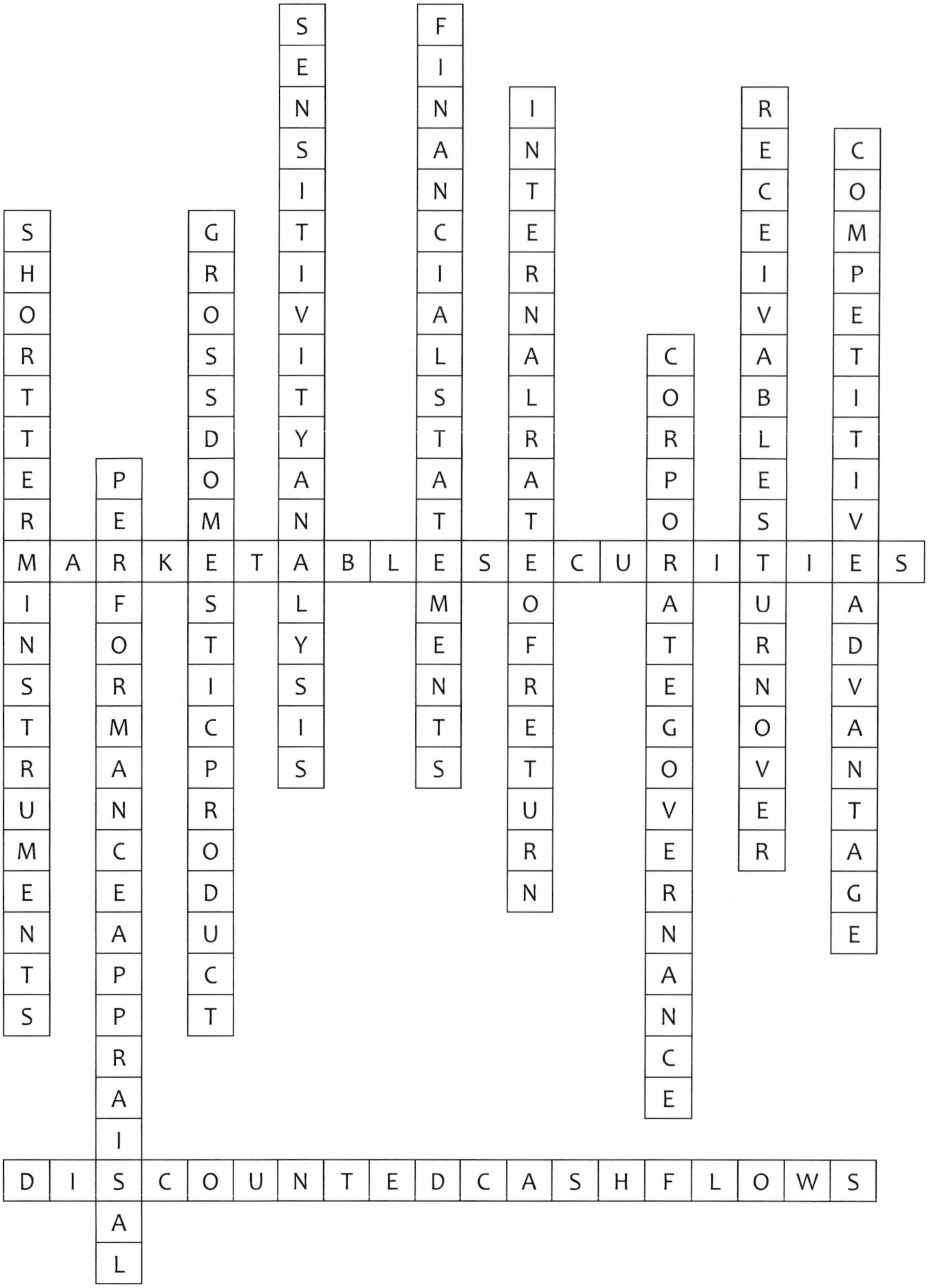
SHORTTERMINSTRUMENTS
PERFORMANCEAPPRAISAL
GROSSDOMESTICPRODUCT
SENSITIVITYANALYSIS
FINANCIALSTATEMENTS
INTERNALRATEOFRETURN
CORPORATEGOVERNANCE
RECEIVABLESTURNOVER
COMPETITIVEADVANTAGE
MARKETABLESECURITIES
DISCOUNTEDCASHFLOWS

Twenty-Ones Plus

Across:
- SUSTAINABLE GROWTH RATE
- CORPORATE SOCIAL RESPONSIBILITY
- CRITICAL SUCCESS FACTORS
- ACCUMULATED DEPRECIATION
- WEIGHTED AVERAGE COST OF CAPITAL

Down:
- GREERHAND... (vertical: G E E R H A N D D E V E L O P M E N T)
- TOTAL QUALITY MANAGEMENT
- CONTINUOUS IMPROVEMENT
- OTHER COMPREHENSIVE INCOME
- KEY PERFORMANCE INDICATORS
- CAPITAL ASSET PRICING MODEL
- ENTERPRISE RISK MANAGEMENT
- BREAK EVEN ANALYSIS
- MANAGEMENT LETTER OF MEANINGFM...
- MANAGEMENT FM (MANAGEMENT ...)
- REVENUE RECOGNITION SYSTEM
- NONCONTROLLING INTEREST
- BOSTON CONSULTING GROUP

Find the Word

Threes and Fours	Booth
Fives and Sixes	Insead
Sevens and Eights	London
Nines	Kellogg
Tens	Wharton
Elevens	Harvard
Twelves	Stanford
Thirteens and Fourteens	Columbia
Fifteens and Sixteens	Manchester
Seventeens Plus	Ross

Please send your feedback, comments, or suggestions to: basel@busiword.com